Anonymous

Church of the Pilgrims

The order of public worship, confession of faith, covenant, forms of admission, etc., ecclesiastical principles and rules : with a list of the members, to 1869

Anonymous

Church of the Pilgrims
The order of public worship, confession of faith, covenant, forms of admission, etc., ecclesiastical principles and rules : with a list of the members, to 1869

ISBN/EAN: 9783337037796

Printed in Europe, USA, Canada, Australia, Japan

Cover: Foto ©Lupo / pixelio.de

More available books at **www.hansebooks.com**

The Church of the Pilgrims.

THE

Order of Public Worship,

CONFESSION OF FAITH,

Covenant, Forms of Admission, Etc.,

Ecclesiastical Principles and Rules:

WITH A

LIST OF THE MEMBERS,

TO 1869.

Officers of the Church.

1869.

PASTOR.
RICHARD S. STORRS, Jr.; Installed November 19th, 1846.

DEACONS.
ELI MYGATT, Jr. .... Term expires, Jan., 1871.
ARCHIBALD BAXTER .... Term expires, Jan., 1871.
JOHN C. BARNES, ... Term expires, Jan., 1873.
RICHARD P. BUCK, ... Term expires, Jan., 1873.
DWIGHT JOHNSON, ... Term expires, Jan., 1875.
COE ADAMS, ... Term expires, Jan., 1875.

EXAMINING COMMITTEE.
RICHARD S. STORRS, Jr. .... CHAIRMAN, *ex-officio*.
JAMES P. WALLACE, ... Term expires, Jan., 1870.
ARCHIBALD BAXTER .... Term expires, Jan., 1870.
RICHARD P. BUCK, ... Term expires, Jan., 1871.
DWIGHT JOHNSON, ... Term expires, Jan., 1871.
ELI MYGATT, Jr., ... Term expires, Jan., 1872.
LUCIEN BIRDSEYE, ... Term expires, Jan., 1872.

TREASURER.
SAMUEL F. PHELPS.

CLERK.
JOHN C. BARNES.

Officers of the Sunday School.

1869.

Superintendent	JAMES H. STORRS.
Vice Superintendent	S. B. CHITTENDEN Jr.
Treasurer	SAMUEL C. SELDEN.
Secretary	CHARLES A. WALLACE.
Librarian	ALBERT G. ALLEN, Jr.

Officers of the Society, 1869.

TRUSTEES.

Archibald Baxter, Joshua M. Van Cott, Anthony Gilkison,	Term expires, April, 1869.
Dwight Johnson, Sidney Green, Walter T. Hatch,	Term expires, April, 1870.
George L. Nichols, Frederick R. Fowler, Albert Woodruff,	Term expires, April, 1871.

Officers of the Board.

Dwight Johnson, President.   W. T. Hatch, Sec'y and Treas.

Standing Committee.

Dwight Johnson, *ex-officio*.   Sidney Green.

Frederick R. Fowler.

Pew Committee.

Walter T. Hatch.   George L. Nichols.

Music Committee.

George L. Nichols.   Archibald Baxter.

Members of the Church.

Received, from the beginning, on Confession of Faith.............415
Received, on Letters from other Churches......................821

    Total..1236

Dismissed, to other Churches.....................................521
Died..107
Watch and Discipline withdrawn....................................3
Excommunicated..1

    Total...632

MEMBERS, JANUARY, 1869.

Male,...233
Female,...371

    Total...604

COMMUNION SUNDAYS.

The first Sunday in January, March, May, July, October, and November. Baptism of children, ordinarily, on the morning of the same days.

BUSINESS MEETINGS OF THE CHURCH.

On the Friday Evening preceding the first Sunday in each month. The Annual Meeting, in January.

Schedule of Annual Contributions.

JANUARY: American Home Missionary Society.
    S. F. PHELPS, J. C. ATWATER, } Committee.

FEBRUARY: Brooklyn City Bible Society.
    S. SANDERSON, J. C. BARNES, } Committee.

MARCH: Cong. Union, and Board of Publication.
    C. B. DAVENPORT, G. B. DOUGLAS, } Committee.

APRIL: Cause of Christian Education.
    COE ADAMS, E. MYGATT, JR., } Committee.

MAY: American Seaman's Friend Society.
    R. P. BUCK, B. F. SHERMAN, } Committee.

JUNE: American and Foreign Christian Union.
    C. B. CALDWELL, R. S. BUSSING, } Committee.

JULY: Children's Aid Society.
    W. C. STREET, H. L. BREVOORT, } Committee.

SEPTEMBER: American Tract Society.
    T. HINSDALE, MARTIN N. DAY, } Committee.

OCTOBER: American Board, for Foreign Missions.
    F. R. FOWLER, A. BAXTER, } Committee.

NOVEMBER: Brooklyn City Mission and Tract Society.
    D. JOHNSON, M. D. THOMAS, } Committee.

DECEMBER: American Sunday-School Union.
    A. WOODRUFF, JAMES H. STORRS, } Committee.

On the occasion of the ANNUAL THANKSGIVING, a Collection is taken in behalf of the Poor connected with the Mission Schools.

Order of Public Worship.

MORNING SERVICE.

I. AFTER a suitable prelude on the organ, the first measures of the tune Old Hundred are played, and the congregation rise, without notice from the Minister, and sing the DOXOLOGY:

> Praise God, from whom all blessings flow:
> Praise Him, all creatures here below:
> Praise Him above, ye Heavenly Host:
> Praise Father, Son, and Holy Ghost.

II. THE PRAYER OF INVOCATION is offered by the Minister, [the congregation bowing down.]

III. THE OPENING HYMN is read by the Minister, and sung by the choir and congregation, [all standing.]

IV. A portion of THE HOLY SCRIPTURE is read by the Minister, [the congregation sitting.]

V. THE PRAYER OF GENERAL SUPPLICATION is offered by the Minister, [the congregation bowing down;] and at the close of it is repeated, by both Minister and people, THE LORD'S PRAYER:

> OUR FATHER, WHO ART IN HEAVEN,
> HALLOWED BE THY NAME.
> THY KINGDOM COME.
> THY WILL BE DONE ON EARTH,
> AS IT IS IN HEAVEN.
> GIVE US THIS DAY OUR DAILY BREAD.
> AND FORGIVE US OUR TRESPASSES,
> AS WE FORGIVE THOSE WHO TRESPASS AGAINST US.
> AND LEAD US NOT INTO TEMPTATION;
> BUT DELIVER US FROM EVIL:
> FOR THINE IS THE KINGDOM,
> AND THE POWER, AND THE GLORY,
> FOREVER AND EVER. AMEN.

VI. A Lesson from THE PSALTER is announced by the Minister, and is read by him and the congregation responsively, [all standing;] and at the close thereof is sung, by the choir and the congregation the ancient DOXOLOGY:

> Glory be to the Father, and to the Son, and to the Holy Ghost; as it was in the beginning, is now, and ever shall be, world without end. Amen.

VII. After these acts of Prayer and Praise [the congregation having resumed their seats,] any NOTICES may be given by the Minister, of religious meetings for the week to come, or of other matters suitable to be brought on the Lord's Day to the knowledge of the Church; and then

VIII. A HYMN, or CHANT, announced, but not read by the Minister, is sung by the choir, [the congregation still sitting.]

IX. This is followed by THE SERMON.

X. After the Sermon, the CLOSING HYMN is read or announced by the Minister, and is sung by the choir and the congregation, [all standing.]

XI. THE PRAYER FOR A BLESSING ON THE WORD is offered by the Minister; and at the end of it [while the congregation are still bowed down,] he pronounces THE BENEDICTION:

> The grace of our Lord Jesus Christ, and the love of God, and the communion of the Holy Ghost, be with you all. Amen.

NOTE.—When Children are to be baptized, they must be presented for that ordinance at the Morning Service, on the proper Sundays, immediately after THE PRAYER OF INVOCATION.

When Collections are to be taken for charitable objects, they may follow either the NOTICES, or the SERMON, at the discretion of the Minister.

EVENING SERVICE.

I. After a suitable prelude on the organ, a brief CHANT or ANTHEM is sung by the choir, [the congregation sitting.]

II. THE OPENING HYMN is read by the Minister, and sung by the choir and the congregation, [all standing.]

III. A portion of THE HOLY SCRIPTURE is read by the Minister, [the congregation sitting.]

IV. THE PRAYER OF GENERAL SUPPLICATION is offered by the Minister, [the congregation bowing down.]

V. A Lesson from THE PSALTER is announced by the Minister, and is read by him and the congregation responsively, [all standing;] and at the close thereof is sung, by the choir and the congregation, the ancient DOXOLOGY:

> Glory be to the Father, and to the Son, and to the Holy Ghost; as it was in the beginning, is now, and ever shall be, world without end. Amen.

VI. After these acts of Prayer and Praise [the congregation having resumed their seats,] any NOTICES may be given by the Minister, of religious meetings for the week to come, or of other matters suitable to be brought on the Lord's Day to the knowledge of the Church; and then

VII. A HYMN, or CHANT, announced, but not read by the Minister, is sung by the choir, [the congregation still sitting.]

VIII. This is followed by THE SERMON.

IX. After the Sermon, the CLOSING HYMN is read or announced by the Minister, and is sung by the choir and congregation, [all standing.] At the end of this hymn a DOXOLOGY, in the same metre, is usually added.

X. THE PRAYER FOR A BLESSING ON THE WORD is offered by the Minister; and at the end of it [while the congregation are still bowed down,] he pronounces THE BENEDICTION:

> The grace of our Lord Jesus Christ, and the love of God, and the communion of the Holy Ghost, be with you all. Amen.

COMMUNION SERVICE.

AFTER a brief prelude on the organ, and a few sentences from the Psalms read by the Minister,

I. THE OPENING HYMN is read or announced, and is sung by the choir and the congregation, [all standing.]

II. A suitable portion of THE HOLY SCRIPTURE is read by the Minister, [the congregation sitting.]

III. THE PRAYER OF CONFESSION AND INVOCATION is offered by the Minister, [the congregation bowing down.]

IV. Any persons who are to be received to the Church on Confession of Faith, are then received, according to the FORM provided in the Manual.

V. Any persons who are to be received to the Church on Letters from other Churches, are then received, according to the FORM provided in the Manual.

VI. Any NOTICES, necessary to be given, are read; and an INVITATION is extended to Christians present, to commune with the Church.

VII. A SACRAMENTAL HYMN is read by the Minister, and sung by the choir and congregation, [all standing.]

VIII. This is followed by a brief ADDRESS.

IX. THE PRAYER FOR THE DIVINE BLESSING, on those who partake of the consecrated elements, is offered by the Minister, [the congregation bowing down;] and the BREAD is afterward broken and distributed.

X. THE PRAYER OF THANKSGIVING is offered by the Minister, [the congregation bowing down;] and the CUP is afterward distributed.

XI. The COLLECTION for the relief of the Poor is taken; during which the Minister reads Sentences from the Scripture.

XII. THE CLOSING HYMN is read by the Minister, and sung by the choir and the congregation, [all standing.]

XIII. THE CLOSING PRAYER is offered by the Minister; and at the end of it [while the congregation are still bowed down,] he pronounces THE BENEDICTION.

The Confession of Faith.

We believe that there is but One God, the Creator, the Preserver, and the Governor of the Universe; a Being self-existent and immutable, infinite in power, wisdom, justice, goodness, mercy, and truth.

We believe that The Scriptures, of the Old and New Testaments, were given by inspiration of God, and are a perfect rule of faith and practice.

We believe that God is revealed in the Scriptures, as The Father and the Son and the Holy Ghost; that these three are One God, and in all divine attributes equal.

We believe that God made all things, and that known unto Him are all His works from the beginning; that He governs all things, according to the counsel of His will; and that the principles and administration of His Government are perfectly holy, just, and good.

We believe that man was originally Holy; that he fell from this happy state, by sinning against God; that, in consequence of this fall, mankind are by nature wholly inclined to sin, destitute of holiness, and alienated from God, and do so continue until renewed and reconciled, through Christ, by the influence of the Spirit.

We believe that God, as an act of mere mercy, gave His Son to die for the sins of the world; and that Jesus Christ, by his obedience, sufferings, and death, has made an Atonement, sufficient for the redemption of all mankind; so that pardon and Eternal Life are sincerely offered to all, upon condition of repentance and faith in the Lord Jesus Christ.

We believe that mankind, of their own accord, do refuse to comply with these conditions, to the aggravation of their guilt

and condemnation; but that God, notwithstanding, did alway purpose to save from deserved ruin great multitudes of the human race, through sanctification by the Spirit, and belief of the truth.

We believe that without a change of heart, by the special agency of the Holy Spirit, no one becomes an heir of Eternal Life.

We believe that the influence of the Holy Spirit is bestowed, not as the reward of antecedent merit or well-doing on the part of him who receives it, but as THE FREE GIFT OF GOD; yet that it is ordinarily so connected with the use of means by the sinner, as creates entire obligation and ample encouragement to attend upon these, and renders all hope of conversion in the neglect of them most presumptuous.

We believe in the necessity of such repentance for sin as arises from supreme love to God; and of such faith in Jesus Christ as includes an affectionate submission to Him, and reliance upon Him for pardon and Eternal Life; and that those who truly believe in Him will be kept, by the mighty power of God, through faith, unto SALVATION.

We believe that there will be a RESURRECTION OF THE DEAD, both of the just and of the unjust; that all must stand before the Judgment Seat of Christ, and receive a sentence of retribution, according to deeds done in the body; and that the wicked will go into punishment, but the righteous into life, both of which will be without end.

Moreover, We believe that in this world the Lord Jesus Christ has A VISIBLE CHURCH; in which the terms of membership are a public profession of faith in Christ, sustained by credible evidence; that its special ordinances are BAPTISM and the LORD'S SUPPER; that these are to be observed in the Church to the end of the world; that none but those who are members of Christ by a living faith, and who have confessed that faith before men, have a right to partake of the Lord's Supper; and that only Believers, and their infant children, are proper subjects for the ordinance of Baptism.

The Covenant.

WE severally avouch THE LORD JEHOVAH, Father, Son, and Holy Ghost, to be OUR GOD, the object of our supreme affection, and our portion forever. We cordially acknowledge THE LORD JESUS CHRIST to be our Redeemer, and THE HOLY SPIRIT our Sanctifier, Comforter, and Guide. We cheerfully devote ourselves to God, in the everlasting covenant of His grace, consecrating all our powers and faculties to His service and glory. And we promise, that through the assistance of His Spirit, by faith in Christ, we will cleave to Him as our chief good; that we will give diligent attention to His WORD and ORDINANCES; that we will seek the honor and interest of His KINGDOM; and that henceforth, denying all ungodliness and every worldly lust, we will live soberly, righteously, and godly, in the world.

We do also cordially join ourselves to this Church, and engage to submit to its rules of government and discipline; to strive earnestly for its purity, peace, and edification; and to walk with all its members in charity and faithfulness, in meekness and sobriety.

Form for the Admission of Members,

UPON CONFESSION OF FAITH.

The names of those who desire to enter the Church, upon Confession of their Faith, having been read, they present themselves before the Table of the Lord, and the Minister addresses them as follows:

BELOVED FRIENDS: The act you now perform is great and solemn, and in its influence will be eternal. The vows which you have made in secret, you here, in public, are to confess and ratify. Within these walls, which have been dedicated to God; before these human witnesses of your faith; beneath that cloud of unseen spirits, whose hearts rejoice at your repentance; under the view of Him who died, but who now liveth forevermore, your risen Lord; you come, to take Christ's vows upon you, to own yourselves His glad disciples, to enter communion and fellowship with His Church. The Spiritual World draws near us, therefore. Immortal relations surround the hour. This scene of your Confession shall stand again before your thoughts, when you are called to sit with Christ, and all the holy, at His marriage-supper. The truths, the purposes, you now declare, shall be your joy, if you are His, when Heaven hath opened its vision and reward. In God, let your whole trust be placed. With faithful, firm, and reverent hearts, devote yourselves to Him: and His rich grace shall keep and bless you!

The following is the summary of Christian Doctrine, adopted by this Church:

[*Here read the Confession of Faith.*]

Do you severally assent to these articles of belief?

You will then publicly, amid this visible and that Unseen Presence, renew your Covenant with God:

[*Here read the Covenant.*]

Do you thus devote yourselves, to be the Lord's?

[*Those who have not been baptized will here receive the Sacrament of Baptism.*]

Most affectionately, now, do we, the Members of this Church, receive you thus to our communion.

[*Here all members of the Church rise, to signify their participation in the welcome given to those who are received.*]

With praising hearts, we own you, from this hour, our kindred in Christ. We welcome you to all the ordinances which mark this house the House of God. We break with you this Bread of Life. We share with you this Cup of Blessing. We ask your aid in turning to our Master the souls of others. And, on our part, we covenant with you, to gird you with our sympathies; to offer for you our prayers; to walk with you, in sorrow or in joy, while you are with us, as Christian friends, seeking advice and strength from you, and giving in return the counsel and the aid which you may ask. We promise to hold your peace and welfare as our own; gladly to render our offices of love; and in all ways, so far as in us lies, to seek your growth in knowledge and in grace, your sweet and calm experience of Christ's love, your perfect meetness for the Heavenly Home!

BELOVED: THE LORD BLESS YOU, AND KEEP YOU: THE LORD MAKE HIS FACE SHINE UPON YOU, AND BE GRACIOUS UNTO YOU: THE LORD LIFT UP HIS COUNTENANCE UPON YOU, AND GIVE YOU PEACE! AMEN.

Form for the Admission of Members,

FROM OTHER CHURCHES.

The names of those who have presented letters from other Churches having been read, they rise, in their several places, and the Minister addresses them, as follows:

BELOVED FRIENDS: Presenting yourselves for union with this Church, upon this day which Christ hath chosen, amid the scenes of this communion, you in effect renew your vows as the disciples of the Saviour. Before our Father, whose eye is on us; before this witnessing assembly of His children; before the unseen communion of the Just; you again confess CHRIST, as your Teacher and Friend, your Divine Master, and your only Redeemer. You acknowledge union with Him to be your joy and hope, and to His service you freshly devote yourselves, with all that hath been given you.

You accept the Confession of Faith adopted by this Church, and declare your belief of the doctrines which it contains.

You do also cordially unite yourselves to this Church, and engage to submit to its rules and discipline; to labor for its purity, its peace, and its advancement; with the grace of God assisting you, to be to it ensamples of the spirit of Christ; and to walk with all its members in faithfulness and meekness, and in the confidence of love. This, you promise?

We, then, the Members and the Minister of this Church, most affectionately receive you to our communion.

[*Here all members of the Church rise, to signify their welcome.*]

We welcome you to this fellowship with us, in the enjoyment of the Gospel, and in the labors for its spread. And we promise, on our part, to watch over you, in love and with fidelity; to surround you with our sympathies; to remember you in our prayers; to commune with you of our Saviour; and to seek continually your meetness for Heaven. And may the God of peace, that brought again from the dead our Lord Jesus, that Great Shepherd of the sheep, through the blood of the everlasting covenant, make you PERFECT, in every good work, to do His will; working in you, and us, that which is well-pleasing in His sight, through Jesus Christ: to whom be glory, for ever and ever. Amen!

Form for the Baptism of Children.

Immediately after the Invocation, at the opening of the Morning Service, on the appointed Sunday, an invitation is given to parents to present their children for Baptism. While they are coming forward, an appropriate chant is sung by the choir. At the close of the chant, the Minister addresses the parents, as follows:

You, who now present your children, to receive upon them the seal of God's covenant, confess yourselves believers in God and in His Son, and in the verity and the continuance of His promise to His children, to be a Father to them, and to their seed after them. You covenant, on your part, in the presence of God, and of these witnesses, to train these children, whom He hath given you, in the nurture and admonition of the Lord; to instruct them in the knowledge of all Divine Truth, as you may have opportunity, but especially in the way of salvation through Jesus Christ; to walk before them daily, as God may give you grace, in the cheerful and holy beauty of the Christian life; to seek, as your chief end concerning them, their renewal of heart, and their salvation in the Redeemer; and to labor, in all ways, with devout and prayerful endeavor, to prepare them to accomplish God's will on earth, and to enter His rest and glory in the skies. DO YOU THUS PROMISE?

As the Minister of Christ, then, I baptize them, into the name of the Creator, the Redeemer, and the Sanctifier of Men:

After the children have been baptized, prayer is offered by the Minister; and another chant is sung by the choir, as the parents, at the close of the prayer, withdraw.

[The name of the child must be given to the Minister in writing, with the date of its birth, and the names of its parents.]

Form for the Solemnization of Marriage.*

At the time appointed, the persons to be married standing together, the man on the right hand, and the woman on the left, the Minister says:

Our help is in the name of the Lord, who made heaven and earth.

Blessed is every one that feareth the Lord; that walketh in his ways.

Let all those that put their trust in thee rejoice; let them ever shout for joy, because thou defendest them; let them also that love thy name be joyful in thee.

For the Lord is good; his mercy is everlasting; and his truth endureth to all generations.

DEARLY BELOVED: We are gathered together here, in the sight of God, and in the presence of these witnesses, to join together this man and this woman in the bonds of Marriage; which is an honorable estate, instituted of God in the time of man's innocency, and afterward blessed, hallowed, and adorned by the Son of God, in his presence, and the first miracle that he wrought, in Cana of Galilee; which is commended in the Holy Scripture as honorable among all men, and by which is clearly signified unto us the mystical union between Christ and his Church; which is not, therefore, to be entered into unadvisedly or lightly, but reverently, discreetly, with gratitude to God, and in humble dependence upon his favor.

* This is the order used in the Marriage-service, by the Pastor of this Church. It is inserted here for the convenience of those who may wish to refer to it.

Into this estate of Marriage these two persons, —— and ——, come now to be joined. Therefore, if any man can show just cause why they may not lawfully be joined together, let him now speak, or else forever hold his peace.

Also, speaking unto the persons who are to be married, the Minister says:

I require and charge you both, as ye will answer at the dreadful day of Judgment, when the secrets of all hearts shall be disclosed, that if either of you know any impediment, why you may not lawfully be joined together, ye do now confess it. For be ye well assured that if any are joined otherwise than as God's word doth allow, their marriage is not lawful.

If no impediment be alleged, then the Minister says:

Who giveth this woman to be married to this man?

And, receiving her at the hand of her father, or other friend, he causes the man with his right hand to take the woman by her right hand, and proposes to each, in turn, the Marriage Covenant, as follows:

Dost thou, ——, take this woman whom thou holdest by the hand to be thy only wedded Wife, to live with her after God's ordinance, in the blessed estate of Christian Marriage?

The man shall answer:

I do.

Wilt thou love her, cherish her, honor and keep her, in sickness or in health, in want or in wealth, and forsaking all other keep thee only unto her, so long as ye both shall live upon the earth?

The man shall answer:

I will.

God's ordinance, in the blessed estate of Christian Marriage?

The woman shall answer:

I do.

Wilt thou love him, succor him, honor and keep him, in sickness or in health, in want or in wealth, and forsaking all other keep thee only unto him, so long as ye both shall live upon the earth?

The woman shall answer:

I will.

For better, for worse, for richer, for poorer, for sickness or health, until death shall you part, you, who have joined your hands together, do take each other, as Wife and as Husband, from this day forward, to love and to cherish each the other, and to dwell in mutual charity and help. Thereto, then, by giving and receiving a ring, you each to the other plight your troth.

The ring shall be handed by the man to the Minister, who holding it says:

This ring, as the gifts of Isaac to Rebekah, is the sign between you of the vows you have made, the pledge of love and a constant fidelity, the symbol of an endless bond.

It shall then be returned by him to the man, who shall place it on the fourth finger of the woman's left hand; and the Minister then makes declaration of the Marriage, as follows:

Forasmuch as —— and —— have consented together in Christian wedlock, and have witnessed the same before God and this company, and thereto have engaged and plighted their troth, each to the other, by joining hands, and by publicly giving and receiving a ring, I pronounce them Husband and Wife; no longer twain, but now one; married, according to the ordinance of God; in the name of the Father, and of

the Son, and of the Holy Ghost. And those whom God hath joined together let not man put asunder.

Then a prayer is offered, for the Divine blessing; closing with this Benediction:

God, the Father, the Son, and the Holy Ghost, bless, preserve, and keep you; the Lord mercifully with his favor regard you, and fill you with all spiritual benediction and grace; that ye may so live together, in this present time, that in the world to come ye shall have life everlasting.

The grace of the Lord Jesus Christ, and the love of God, and the communion of the Holy Ghost, be with you all. AMEN.

[The names of the parties must always be given to the Minister in full, in writing; with the names of two persons, present at the marriage. This is for the Record, and for the Certificate.]

Ecclesiastical Principles and Rules.

I. RIGHTS OF THE CHURCH.—This Church regards the Scriptures as the only infallible guide in matters of church order and discipline; and is, therefore, so far as relates to its internal organization and the regulation of its affairs, independent, and amenable to no other ecclesiastical body, except by its own consent, and in accordance with established Congregational principles. With these exceptions, it controls the admission, discipline, and removal of its members, according to its own understanding of the Word of God.

II. CONNECTION WITH OTHER CHURCHES.—This Church will extend to other evangelical Congregational Churches, and receive from them, that fellowship, advice, and assistance, which the laws of Christ require. It will extend the usual rights of communion, and practice the usual transfer of members, according to its conviction of duty. It holds itself bound to regard the decisions of Mutual Councils, and to seek the promotion of peace with all the Churches of our Lord Jesus Christ.

III. ADMISSION OF MEMBERS.—All persons who desire to make a profession of religion, and to unite with this Church, shall be examined by the Examining Committee, before such members of the Church as desire to be present. The names of such as are approved shall be propounded to the Church, in the presence of the congregation, at least one week previous to their admission; and they shall become members by a vote of the Church, on signing the Confession of Faith and Covenant, and giving public assent to the same,—receiving the sacrament of Baptism if they have not been before baptized.

Members of other churches, submitting the proper testimonials to the Examining Committee, shall be conferred with by them; and if approved, shall be also propounded before the congregation for one week, and be received, by a vote of the Church, on signing the Confession of Faith, and publicly entering into covenant with the Church.

A member who may know of any reason why a candidate for admission should not be received into this Church, shall first make such reason known to the Examining Committee, and not to the whole Church, unless the Committee refuse so to do when requested by him; as in cases of complaint against members, specified in Article VI.

IV. DISMISSION OF MEMBERS.—This Church will, by its vote, grant letters of dismission and recommendation to its members in regular standing. All applications should be made in writing, and referred to the Examining Committee, who shall report upon them at the next regular meeting of the Church after they are so referred; and all such letters of recommendation and dismission shall be signed by the Clerk, and shall purport to be valid for one year only from the date thereof. Letters shall not be granted to persons who have delayed applying for them for more than one year after their removal, unless special reasons, satisfactory to the Church, shall be assigned for such delay.

V. MEMBERS OF OTHER CHURCHES.—It is expected that any members of other Churches, who may wish to commune with this Church for more than one year, will request dismission from their respective Churches, and admission to this, unless they assign reasons for the delay satisfactory to the Examining Committee.

VI. RIGHTS OF MEMBERS.—Every member has a right to Church privileges, unless forfeited by misconduct; and when thus forfeited, he can be deprived of them only by regular process. The presentation of complaints shall in all cases be first made to the Examining Committee, who shall, upon sufficient cause, prefer charges before the whole Church. And in case the Committee refuse so to do, the complainant may nevertheless if he insist upon the charges, present his complaint in person to the Church.

When a member is accused, he shall be seasonably furnished with a copy of the complaint, and shall have a full hearing. While the trial is pending, the accused is expected to abstain from participating in the Lord's Supper.

VII. DUTIES OF THE CHURCH AND ITS MEMBERS.—It is the duty of the members to attend such stated meetings as are appointed by a vote of the Church, unless providentially prevented.

Any member having cause of complaint against another, should immediately seek to have it removed, in a Christian manner; the directions given in Matthew 18: 15-17, being his guide, especially in cases of personal offense.

Any member wishing to withdraw from this Church, and to unite with another, should signify his wishes and his reasons, and apply to be first released from his obligations to this Church. Any other mode of withdrawal will be deemed irregular and censurable; and this Church holds itself bound to grant to its members, in regular standing, letters of dismission and recommendation to churches, not only of our own, but of any other evangelical denomination.

VIII. CENSURABLE OFFENSES.—This Church considers immoral conduct, breach of express covenant vows, neglect of acknowledged religious or relative duties, and avowed disbelief of the articles of faith to which the members have assented, as offenses, subject to the censure of the Church.

IX. CENSURES.—The censures to be inflicted on offenders are, private reproof, public admonition, the withdrawal of the watch and discipline of the Church, or excommunication, according to the aggravation of the offense. In case of excommunication, notice thereof shall be given from the pulpit on the Sabbath.

Standing Rules.

1. The stated officers of this Church shall be the Pastor or Pastors, Deacons, Stated Clerk, and Treasurer. To the Pastor pertains the office of Moderator.

2. The standing committees of this Church shall be the Examining Committee, and such other committees as shall be chosen for one year, or any longer term.

3. All meetings for business shall be opened with prayer.

4. A meeting for the choice of officers and standing committees, and for other business, shall be held annually in the month of January. At this, the records of the last year shall be read, the catalogue of members revised, and accounts presented by the Treasurer of all monies received, expended, or held by him, on behalf of the Church, during the year—which accounts shall be duly audited, by persons appointed for that purpose, and be placed on file by the Clerk.

5. A regular meeting of the Church shall be held after the religious services on the Friday evening next preceding the first Sabbath in each month; but at the meeting next before each Communion, no business except the reception and dismission of members shall be transacted, unless by a suspension of this rule.

6. The Annual and other Regular Meetings of the Church, for the transaction of business, shall be announced from the pulpit on the preceding Sabbath.

7. Special meetings may be called by the Pastor, or by a majority of the Deacons, or by the Clerk at the written request of seven male members of lawful age; but in the last case, notice shall be given from the pulpit on the Sabbath, as in case of a regular meeting.

8. Standing committees and officers shall be elected by ballot, without nomination; and all elections shall be determined by the vote of a majority of male members of lawful age, present and voting, at a meeting notified in accordance with the preceding rules.

9. The Examining Committee shall consist of the Pastor, who shall be

a permanent member, and of six other members of the Church, whose election and term of office shall be as follows:

At the Annual Meeting in 1847, two members shall be chosen for one year, two for two years, and two for three years; and at every subsequent Annual Meeting, two members shall be chosen for three years, in place of those whose term of office will then expire.

10. Vacancies in any of the offices or standing committees occurring between the Annual Meetings may be filled at the next Annual Meeting, or at any regular business meeting of the Church—notice of the intention to fill such vacancies having been given from the pulpit on the three successive Sabbaths next preceding such meeting; and the person appointed to the vacancy shall hold the office for the unexpired term wherein he shall be elected.

11. It shall be the duty of the Stated Clerk to give notice to the Church of vacancies in any of the stated offices or committees, at the next regular business meeting after their occurrence; in order that, if the Church shall so direct, such vacancy may be filled, in accordance with the preceding rule.

12. It shall also be the duty of the Stated Clerk to keep a record, containing minutes of the doings of the Church, with the Covenant, Confession of Faith, Forms of Admission, Ecclesiastical Principles and Rules, and Standing Rules, recorded in a place by themselves; and a Chronological List of the Members, with the time of their admission, dismission, or death, so far as he can ascertain the same.

13. It shall be the duty of the Examining Committee to examine all applicants for admission to the Church, and to make a written report of such as they deem suitable candidates. They shall also report to the Church the names of such members as have removed from the city, their place of residence, and the length of time since their removal; together with any other information respecting them, which they may think it important to communicate.

14. It shall be the duty of the Deacons to assist in the administration of the Lord's Supper, to distribute the charities of the Church, to minister especially to such of the congregation as are poor or in any affliction, to preside at religious meetings of the Church for which provision is not otherwise made, and, in the absence or at the request of the Pastor, to provide a supply for the pulpit. The term of office of the Deacons shall be limited to six years.

15. The Lord's Supper shall be celebrated on the first Sabbath of January, March, May, July, October, and November. The admission of members, together with the celebration of this ordinance, shall constitute the services of the afternoon.

16. The Sacrament of Baptism shall be administered to the children of believers, ordinarily, on the morning of the Communion Sabbath; and to adults, after they have publicly professed faith in Christ, and before their approach to the Table of the Lord.

To each child baptized in this Church, whose parents shall continue connected with it till the child has reached the age of seven years, shall be then presented by the Church a copy of the Holy Scriptures, with the name of the child, and the dates of its birth and its baptism, inscribed therein.

17. A contribution shall be made at every Communion-service; and the fund thus obtained shall be used to defray the current expenses of the Church, and in assisting its necessitous members.

18. The expenses of the delegations of the Church to Ecclesiastical Councils, shall be paid by the Treasurer, from the funds of the Church; and such delegations shall make report of the doings of the Councils to which they have been sent, at the next subsequent meeting of the Church.

19. This Church will meet, for prayer and conference, every Friday evening.

20. The Confession of Faith, Covenant, Forms of Admission, Ecclesiastical Principles and Rules, or Standing Rules, may not be altered, except by a vote of two-thirds of the male members of the Church, of lawful age, present and voting at an Annual Meeting; nor shall such alteration be considered, unless a notice containing the substance thereof has been given in writing at a previous meeting.

Constitution, and By-Laws,

OF THE
SUNDAY-SCHOOL.

ARTICLE I.

This School shall be called THE SUNDAY-SCHOOL OF THE CHURCH OF THE PILGRIMS.

It shall be under the charge and oversight of the Church, and the constant supervision of the PASTOR; who is requested to visit the teachers at their meetings, and the School at its sessions, at least once in every month, and oftener if practicable, and to take such personal part in the instruction as may seem to him desirable.

ARTICLE II.

The officers of the School shall be a Superintendent, a Vice-Superintendent, a Secretary and Treasurer, a Librarian, and an Assistant Librarian, who shall be elected annually, and the term of whose office shall be one year.

ARTICLE III.

It shall be the duty of the Superintendent to preside at the meetings of the Teachers; to take the oversight of the School while in session; to confer with visitors; in the absence of any officer or teacher, to appoint a substitute; and, in general, to use his best endeavors to promote the growth, welfare, and usefulness of the School. He shall be, *ex-officio*, a member of all committees.

ARTICLE IV.

It shall be the duty of the Vice-Superintendent to take the place of the Superintendent, in the absence of the latter.

ARTICLE V.

It shall be the duty of the Secretary to attend each session of the School, and to keep a correct record of all Teachers and Scholars connected with it, with the date of the admission and the removal of each; and to report, at each annual meeting of the Teachers, and of the Church, the condition of the School, the number of its Teachers and Scholars, and their average attendance. He shall also attend the meetings of the Teachers, and record their proceedings.

ARTICLE VI.

It shall be the duty of the Treasurer to receive all monies and donations for the School; to keep a regular and public account of the same; to pay all bills, after the same shall have been approved by the Finance Committee; and to report the condition of the Treasury to the Teachers whenever called upon, and at each annual meeting of the Society.

ARTICLE VII.

It shall be the duty of the Librarian to take charge of the Library, to stamp and number the books contained in it, and to keep a catalogue of the same; to charge each Teacher with the books taken by his or her class; to permit no Scholar to take a second book until the first has been returned; and to report the state of the Library, at each annual meeting of the Teachers and of the Church.

ARTICLE VIII.

It shall be the duty of the Teachers to attend punctually their own meetings, and the sessions of the School; to preserve order and attention among the children under their supervision; and to use their most earnest and prayerful efforts, both by word and by example, to instruct them in religious truth, and to lead them to Christ.

ARTICLE IX.

The Pastor, with the Superintendent and the Vice-Superintendent, shall constitute a COMMITTEE OF CLASSIFICATION AND DISCIPLINE; to which Committee all questions concerning the formation or change of classes, the admission or removal of Teachers and Scholars, and the introduction of Question-books, shall be referred, and by which they shall be decided.

ARTICLE X.

The same persons shall be a COMMITTEE ON THE LIBRARY; by which the lists of books to be purchased for addition to it shall be prepared, and the money appropriated for the same shall be expended; by which also the books displaced from the Library shall be distributed.

ARTICLE XI.

The same persons shall be also a COMMITTEE ON FINANCE; whose duty it shall be to audit all accounts of the Treasurer, and to certify the correctness of all bills to be paid by that officer.

ARTICLE XII.

The Constitution and the By-Laws of the School shall not be changed, except by a vote of the Church, at its Annual Meeting.

By-Laws.

1. The Annual Meeting of the Teachers of the School, for the election of officers, the receiving of Reports, and the transaction of other business, shall be held during the week succeeding the Annual Meeting of the Church. But vacancies occurring in the offices between the Annual Meetings may be filled at any regular meeting of the Teachers, a week's notice having been given of the intention to fill them.

2. In the election of officers of the School, only those Teachers shall be eligible to office, or shall be entitled to vote, who are members of the Church of the Pilgrims, and who have been connected with the School three months previous to the election.

Other Teachers, however, may be placed upon special committees, and shall have a vote upon questions affecting the general administration of the School.

3. A meeting of the Teachers connected with the School shall be held weekly, at the time and place designated by the Superintendent on the previous Sunday, for the purpose of transacting such business as may be necessary, and of studying and discussing the lesson appointed for the next Sunday.

4. If any Teacher shall be prevented from attending a session of the School, it shall be his or her duty to provide a substitute, or to notify the Superintendent, that a substitute may be obtained.

5. The School shall be opened with singing, reading the Scriptures, and prayer; and each session—continuing an hour and a half—shall be closed with singing. There will be no sessions of the School during the months of July and August.

6. Every Scholar is expected to be present, punctually, at the hour appointed for opening the School; to be attentive to the general exercises, as well as to those of his or her particular class; to be obedient to the Teacher, and to conform in all respects to the rules of the School; and no Scholar shall retire before the close of a session, without the permission of the Teacher or of the Superintendent.

7. Special business meetings may be called by the Pastor or Superintendent; or be convened by the Secretary at the call of any three teachers, provided public notice thereof be given to the Teachers, on the Sunday preceding such meeting. And at any business meeting, six Teachers, entitled to vote at an election, shall constitute a quorum.

Members of the Church.

Received December 22, 1844, at the Organization of the Church.

CHARLES B. AHORN.
ALBERT G. ALLEN.
LUCY W. ALLEN.
CHARLOTTE W. ATKINSON, ‖1848.
DAVID F. ATWATER, ‖1855.
GEORGE M. ATWATER, †1852.
CHARLES P. BALDWIN, †1857.
MARY ANN BALDWIN, ‖1857.
MOSES H. BALDWIN, ‖1848.
MARTHA N. BALDWIN, ‖1848.
HIRAM BARNEY, ‖1862.
SUSAN A. BARNEY, ‖1862.
STEPHEN M. BLAKE, †1861.
ELIZABETH ANN BLAKE, ‖1861.
HENRY C. BOWEN, ‖1847.
LUCY M. BOWEN, †1847.
RICHARD P. BUCK.
CHARLOTTE BUCK.
FREDERICK A. BURRALL.
LUCY A. BURRALL, *1846.
STEPHEN E. BURRALL, †1865.
ANN ELWELL DAY, *1857.
SIMEON B. CHITTENDEN.
MARY H. CHITTENDEN, *1852.
ANNA H. CHITTENDEN.
NANCY GOODRIDGE, ‖1850.
JAMES D. HAFF, *1852.
WALTER T. HATCH.
REBECCA T. HATCH.
WHITING H. HOLLISTER, †1852.
SARAH ANN HOLLISTER, †1852.
HORATIO N. HOLT, ‖1855.
ABBY G. HOLT, *1865.
JOHN T. HOWARD, †1847.
SETH B. HUNT, ‖1855.
FRANCES B. HUNT, ‖1855.
AMASA C. LYON, ‖1849.
MARY E. LYON, ‖1849.
THEODORE L. MASON, ‖1862.

KATHARINE VAN V. DE W. MASON, *1859.
CHAUNCEY L. MITCHELL.
CAROLINE L. MITCHELL, ‖1850.
BENJAMIN F. PARSONS, ‖1846.
CHARLES H. PARSONS, ‖1852.
DENNIS PERKINS, ‖1859.
CHARLES ROWLAND, †1847.
MARIA B. ROWLAND, ‖1847.
SYRENA SAWYER, ‖1866.
HEZEKIAH D. SHARPE.
ELIZABETH A. SHARPE.
JOHN SLADE, ‖1855.
LUCY SLADE, ‖1855.
ENOCH C. STANTON, *1851.
LUCY JANE STANTON.
CHARLES J. STEDMAN, *1858.
ELIZABETH S. STEDMAN, *1852.
JOSEPH A. SWEETSER, †1855.
CATHARINE D. SWEETSER, ‖1855.
JEREMIAH P. TAPPAN, †1861.
LYDIA P. TAPPAN, †1861.
LYDIA B. TAPPAN [LANGDON], ‖1860.
MARQUIS D. THOMAS.
LYDIA THOMAS.
WILLIAM VAIL, ‖1846.
CAROLINE VAIL, ‖1846.
GEORGE H. WILLIAMS, ‖1851.
ELIZA M. WILLIAMS, *1848.
SARAH WOODRUFF, *1855.
ALBERT WOODRUFF.
HARRIET WOODRUFF.
CYNTHIA WOODRUFF.

Received in 1845.

SARAH BACKUS, ‖1867.
HARRIET BACKUS [GRIGGS] ‖1867.
JAMES P. BRADLEY, ‖1851.
NANCY BRADLEY, ‖1851.
EDWARD W. COLEMAN, ‖1851.

The notation marks designate as follows: * Died. † Dismissed. ‡ Watch and discipline withdrawn. § Excommunicated.

ANNA DUNCAN [MAXWELL], *1846.
SAMUEL FOSTER, †1861.
REBECCA B. FOSTER, †1861.
NANCY FOSTER, †1861.
HENRY M. GREGORY, †1846.
ELIZABETH GREGORY, †1846.
DAVID GRIFFING, †1847.
ANNA GRIFFING, †1855.
MARY E. HAFF, †1852.
RACHEL KNIGHT, †1847.
LUTHER W. MCFARLAN, †1851.
FRANCES F. MARSH, *1852.
FRANCES MARSH.
LEANDER MOORE, *1850.
HENRY NASON, †1858.
SARAH W. NASON, *1848.
JIRA PAYNE, †1847.
ELIZA PAYNE, †1847.
FRANCES PAYNE, †1847.
SIDNEY SANDERSON.
MARY A. SANDERSON,
CHARLOTTE SANDERSON [QUICK], †1847.
ABIGAIL J. SANDERSON.
CHARLES M. SAXTON, †1853.
SARAH A. C. SAXTON, †1853.
MARY J. SMITH, †1848.
JAMES H. SPELLMAN, †1846.
VERNON THOMPSON, †1847.
HANNAH G. WISE, †1846.

Received in 1846.

JAMES C. ATWATER.
ALFRED S. BARNES, †1855.
HARRIET E. BARNES, †1855.
MARGARET BREWSTER, †1853.
JACOB BRINKERHOFF, JR., †1848.
GAIUS C. BURNAP, †1851.
JANE S. BURNAP, †1851.
EMILY R. CARTWRIGHT.
HARRIET E. CARTWRIGHT [PEASE], †1855.
ROBERT CHURCH.
ELIZA JAMES CHURCH.
GEORGE A. CLARKE, †1852.
ELIZABETH L. CLARKE, *1852.
ELIZABETH L. R. CLARKE, †1852.
JULIA COLLINS, †1851.
ROXANA COLLINS [MOORE], †1851.
JOSEPH H. COLTON, †1858.
ORRILLA C. COLTON, †1858.
GEORGE W. COLTON, $1855.
GEORGE DOMETT, †1848.
AMOS W. GAY, †1852.
JOHN C. HARDY, †1850.
ELIZABETH HULBERT, †1858.
JOHN H. LYMAN, †1851.
SAMUEL F. PHELPS.

PHEBE PHELPS.
MARTHA E. PHELPS [SWIFT], †1866.
ELIJAH PORTER, *1849.
REBECCA PORTER, †1861.
REBECCA A. PORTER, *1856.
MARY A. PORTER, $1855.
PHILO PRICE, †1850.
BETSEY A. PRICE, †1850.
D. WALTER SMITH, $1857.
CLARISSA B. SMITH, *1846.
SAMUEL SWIFT, *1851.
MARY SWIFT, †1858.

Received in 1847.

JOHN A. ACKLEY, *1853.
DELIA ACKLEY, *1859.
CATHARINE E. ACKLEY [SWIFT].
MARCUS ALDEN, *1848.
SALOME H. ALDEN, *1861.
CHARLES M. ATKINSON.
CHRISTINA S. ATWATER.
WILLIAM H. BIGELOW, †1848.
HIRAM BINGHAM, *1851.
JANE E. BINGHAM, †1851.
CHAUNCEY W. BROWN.
JULIA BULKELEY.
LOUISE C. BURGESS [RYDER], †1855.
MARY B. BURRILL, *1865.
CHARLES B. CALDWELL.
CORNELIA W. CANNING, †1854.
VILENDER CARTER, †1856.
LUCIUS E. CLARK, †1868.
ABIGAIL CLARK, †1863.
SARAH W. COOMBS, †1864.
CLARA M. DAVIS, †1864.
JULIA E. DELICKER, †1855.
ELIZABETH P. EVANS, †1851.
ALBERT GATES, †1853.
HARRIET GATES, †1853.
ALONZO GRAY, *1860.
SARAH H. GRAY.
RICHARD G. GREENE, †1856.
MARTHA HAFF, †1850.
CATHARINE HAFF, †1854.
PHEBE HAWLEY, †1849.
JAMES D. HOAG, †1851.
MARY E. HOAG, †1851.
CHARLOTTE S. HOUGH [PERRY], †1856.
JOSHUA HUNTINGTON.
JAMES S. HYDE, *1861.
MARIANNE HYDE.
ALICE JENKS, *1850.
NANCY KING, †1855.
CAROLINE P. KING [HUDSON], †1855.
REUBEN LANGDON, JR., †1860.
MARY URSULA LEAVITT.

Frances M. Lincoln [Rexford], †1851.
John T. Marsh, †1862.
Chauncey W. Moore.
Clara Moore.
Mary Jane Noyes.
William M. Peck.
Eliza Peck.
Maria E. Pratt, *1818.
Elvira Roberts, †1853.
Jeremiah P. Robinson.
Elizabeth Robinson.
Eliza Skeele [Otis], *1868.
Margaret Skeele [Van Wyck], †1849.
Hetty B. Smith, *1856.
James M. Staples, †1861.
Celia T. Staples, *1860.
Chandler Starr, †1855.
Hannah Starr, †1857.
Elizabeth Starr [Ward], †1850.
Sarah A. Starr, †1860.
Richard S. Storrs, Jr.
Mary Elwell Storrs.
Maria L. Thompson [Ropes], †1854.
Chandler B. Trumbull, †1854.
Angelina J. Trumbull, †1854.
James C. Woodruff, †1853.
Elizabeth O. L. Woodruff, †1853.

Received in 1848.

Ephraim Blanchard, †1852.
Elizabeth Blanchard, †1852.
William Beach, †1852.
Julia A. Beach, †1852.
Charles E. Bulkeley, *1853.
Gloriana M. Goggill, †1856.
Isabella Corry, †1858.
Alexander H. Dana, †1867.
Augusta Dana, †1867.
Lucius Field, †1848.
Lucia Field, †1848.
T. W. Grant, †1851.
Eliza A. Grant, †1851.
Andrew T. Hart, †1853.
Harriet B. Hart, †1853.
Ann Grosvenor King, †1860.
Julia King, †1860.
Harriet A. King, †1860.
Susan M. King, †1860.
George Kingsley, †1849.
Mary D. Kingsley, †1849.
Joseph E. Lyman, *1859.
Eliza C. Muir, †1856.
Susan A. Muir [Fisher], †1861.
Elizabeth L. Noyes [Gooch].
Jane Noyes, *1850.
Thomas H. Rodman, †1853.
Mary Ann Rodman, †1853.

William Rust, †1852.
Agnes Sage, †1856.
Hannah Sibley, †1857.
Esther R. Smith [Parsons], †1852.
Elizabeth Smith, *1858.
Mary Smith [Sheldon], †1867.
William P. Warriner, †1853.

Received in 1849.

Cornelia E. Adams [Hobart], †1860.
Emily Burr, †1855.
Samuel Backus, †1861.
William Backus, †1850.
Almira S. Coe, †1856.
Isabella Crozier.
Ellen Colton [Batterson], †1853.
William De Groot, †1851.
Isabella De Groot, †1851.
Jane R. Dana [Noyes], *1858.
Mary Dayton [Rockwell].
Anna Dixon.
William Edwards, *1851.
Rebecca Edwards, *1857.
Nancy M. Farwell, †1852.
William R. Gould, Jr., †1856.
Matilda S. Gould, †1856.
Mary R. Greene.
William A. Hall, *1851.
Susan B. Hall, †1854.
Julia Hart, †1853.
Jesse Hinds, *1859.
Maria Hinds.
Urania Humphrey.
Mary Jacobs [Champney], *1864.
Sarah E. Johnson.
Dwight Johnson.
Mary T. Johnson.
Henry H. King, †1855.
Harriet King.
Laura L. Marsh.
Mary A. Mann, †1853.
Lucy A. Myers, †1856.
Samuel Noyes.
Henrietta J. Noyes.
William C. Noyes, †1853.
Jane R. Noyes, †1853.
Ann M. Parsons [Sanford], †1858.
Hannah M. Perkins, †1859.
Henry C. Perkins, †1859.
Mary Perkins [Slade], *1860.
Robert Perry.
Mary S. Perry.
Margaret Place, *1868.
Caroline E. Porter, †1861.
Harriet L. Porter, †1861.
Ellen M. Porter [Richardson].
Joseph W. Rogers, †1863.

GEORGE ROBERTS, †1853.
CATHARINE E. ROOD, †1854.
GIDEON SANFORD, *1862.
ADELINE R. SANFORD, *1865.
ELIZABETH C. SMITH [GEER], †1855.
FRANCIS H. SLADE, †1852.
JOHN M. SLADE, †1864.
LORENZO SNOW.
JULIET E. SNOW.
ALEXANDER SUTHERLAND, †1865.
JEANETTE SUTHERLAND, †1865.
MARY N. TAPPAN [WHEELWRIGHT].
SUSAN STOREY TAPPAN.
SOPHIA E. TAYLOR, *1851.
AMELIA E. THOMAS.
JANE UNDERWOOD, *1855.
FRANK VINCENT, †1858.
HARRIET B. VINCENT, *1850.

Received in 1850.

EDWARD F. ACKLEY.
BIRDSEY BLAKEMAN, †1857.
ANNA M. BLAKEMAN, †1857.
HORACE CARRUTHERS, †1855*
AMELIA DICKINSON, †1857.
ELLEN M. DICKINSON [DOUBLEDAY], †1857.
CHARLES P. DICKINSON, †1857.
CALEB H. ELY, †1851.
SARAH E. ELY, *1851.
FRANCES E. ELY, †1851.
FANNY ANTILL EDWARDS [ROGERS], †1863.
CHARLES A. FISHER, †1864.
ARETHUSA J. FOX.
STEPHEN S. GOODMAN.
MARY ANN HALSEY, †1851.
SARAH E. HALSEY [MILLER], †1851.
ANN HURLEY, †1858.
WILLIAM ISBISTER, †1853.
PRISCILLA H. JONES.
MARY E. KELLOGG, †1850.
SARAH M. KELLOGG [MCBRIDE], †1866.
DOUGLASS LEFFINGWELL, †1855.
MARIA LECONEY, †1855.
WILLIAM LECONEY, †1855.
SARAH D. LECONEY, †1855.
SARAH E. MERRILL, †1860.
LUCY J. MILLS, †1855.
HENRY M. MCCORKLE, †1854.
CAROLINE M. MCCORKLE, †1854.
ELI MYGATT, JR.
SOPHIA MYGATT.
GEORGE R. NOYES, †1868.
MARGARET PRICE.
ALFRED H. PORTER.
Z. MONTAGUE PHELPS, †1858.   (†1855.)
AMELIA E. RATHBONE [CARRUTHERS],
DANIEL C. RIPLEY, †1865.

SARAH B. RIPLEY, †1865.
MARY W. ROSSITER, †1862.
JOHN RUSSELL, †1852.
ANN RUSSELL, †1852.
MARY SHERWOOD, *1852.
JOHN S. SHERMAN, †1853.
ELIZA B. SHERMAN, †1853.
HENRY C. SHELDON, *1856.
JOHN SLOANE, †1857.
MARY SMITH.
JAMES H. STORRS.
SUSAN F. STORRS.
SARAH STEWART.
HENRY A. UNDERWOOD, †1852.
GEORGE W. VANDERHOVEN, *1851.
GEORGE W. WASHBURN, †1851.
MARGARET M. WEST, †1862.
JOANNA F. WEST [ABBOT], †1862.
SARAH L. WEST [BEEBE], †1851.
WILLIAM W. WICKES, †1857.
JOSEPH WOODBRIDGE, †1851.
CHARLES L. WOODBRIDGE, †1851.
WILLIAM H. WYMAN.

Received in 1851.

JOEL R. ANDREWS, †1860.
REBECCA C. ANDREWS, †1860.
ANN J. ARMSTRONG [ELLIOT], †1858.
MARTIN R. BERRY, †1865.
ELEANOR BERRY, †1865.
ALMIRA E. BUTLER, †1855.
JANE E. CHURCH, *1859.
SARAH A. CHURCH [MOFFATT], †1851.
FRANCIS CHURCH, †1861.
ALMIRA L. CHURCH, †1861.
PHEBE CLARK [MRS.] *1864.
PHEBE CLARK [MISS], †1866.
WILLIAM A. COGGESHALL, †1852.
HARRIET COGGESHALL, †1852.
ELIZABETH COCHRANE, †1854.
ELLEN H. CREECH.
JANE DAY [COLGROVE], †1860.
FRANCIS FISHER.
OLIVER C. GARDINER.
L. ADELINE GARDINER.
A. FRANKLIN GOODNOW.
WELLES HAWES.
ANGELICA A. HAWES.
WILLIAM P. HAWKINS, †1854.
FREDERICK W. HOTCHKISS, †1856.
ELIZA A. HOTCHKISS, †1854.
HENRY R. KIMBERLY, †1863.
O. ADELAIDE KIMBERLY, *1852.
WILLIAM H. LITTLE, †1858.
JOSEPHINE K. LITTLE, †1858.
JAMES MORTON, †1856.
MARY ELIZABETH MORTON, †1856.

Charles A. Nichols, †1860.
William B. Sawyer, †1852.
Julia A. Scammon, †1861.
Hector Sears, †1854.
Susan T. Sears, †1854.
Benjamin P. Sherman.
Almet Skeele, †1858.
Eliza T. Sloane, †1857
Mary Smith, †1854.
Jane Snow.
Michael Snow, †1856.
D. Maria Snow, †1856.
Ann Stewart.
Charles Storrs.
Maryett M. Storrs.
Martha J. Taylor, †1857
Elizabeth Vanderhoven, †1854.

Received in 1852.

Calvin Adams.
Sarah S. Atwater, †1855.
Cornelia C. Atwood [Porter].
William E. Bailey.
Almira P. Baker, †1857.
Olive A. Baker, †1861.
John C. Barnes.
Mary S. Barnes.
Catharine M. Birdseye.
Nathan G. Brown, †1853.
Elizabeth K. Brown, †1854.
Helen Bulkley.
Elizabeth G. Burrill.
Margaret A. Cain.
John S. Carr, †1865.
Timothy P. Chapman, †1858.
Rachel P. Chapman, †1853.
Clinton Clapp.
Julia C. Clarke, †1854
Sumner Clarke, †1856.
Henry M. Crane, †1860.
Louisa F. Crane, †1860.
Francis E. Dana.
William E. Doubleday, †1857.
Thomas Douglass.
Laura Douglass.
Charles Douglass, †1855
Cornelia Douglass, †1855.
Nathan S. Faxon, †1858.
Elizabeth R. Faxon, †1858.
Gilbert H. Ferris, †1868.
Julia A. Heron, †1861.
Joseph H. Higginson, †1853.
Emma B. Higginson, †1853.
John B. Hutchinson, †1857.
Ruthy B. Hutchinson, †1857.
Nathaniel E. James, †1866.

Mary J. James.
D. Willis James, †1855.
Catharine H. Kirby [Burrell].
Charles N. Kinney, †1853.
Margaret E. Kinney, †1853
Frederick A. Lane, †1856
Mary J. Lynde [Babcock], †1854.
Joshua Leavitt.
Sarah Leavitt.
Mary B. Marsh.
Martha Reid.
Catharine W. Ripley, *1865
Katharine W. Ripley [Noyes], †1868.
Eliza C. Ripley.
John L. Ripley, †1855.
Laura Skeele [Hoffmann].
Elizabeth J. Smith.
Caroline Starr [Edwards], †1861.
Frances R. Tappan, †1860.
Albert S. Waite, †1854.
Mary J. West, *1829.
Rebecca J. Wickes, †1857.
Martin H. Williams.
Josiah T. Wright, †1854.
Joseph Woodbridge, †1857.

Received in 1853.

Timothy Atkinson, †1856.
Henrietta Atkinson, †1856.
Mary H. Atkinson, †1856.
Henrietta P. Atkinson, †1856.
Charles Barker, †1855.
Rachel Barker, †1855.
Samuel Bayliss, †1855.
Sarah Bayliss
George A. Clark, †1861.
Rometta L. Clapp, †1857.
Amelia A. Cox [Forman], †1861
Joseph A. Dudley, †1858.
A. Frances Dudley, †1858.
Charlotte Edgerton, †1859.
Samuel Fleet, *1861.
Phebe Fleet, *1855.
Phebe A. Fleet, †1866.
Louise Gregory [Smythe].
Lyman W. Gilbert, †1865.
Isabella Gilbert, †1865.
Joseph M. Hurlburt, †1866
Horace Hunt, †1865.
Aurelius B. Hull.
Sarah T. Hull.
Mabel B. Johns, †1856.
Horace R. Latimer, †1856.
Mary B. Latimer, †1856.
Lucy O. P. Le Breton, †1856.
Caroline F. Little, †1858.

CATALOGUE OF MEMBERS.

Cornelius A. Marvin, †1860.
Ella B. Marvin, †1860.
Emily Matthewson [Olney], †1859.
Caroline L. Mitchell, *1855.
Mary A. Olmstead.
Harriet Pattee, †1862.
John G. Parker, †1854.
Jane Parker, †1854.
Julia E. Parker [Rich], †1854.
William H Penfield, †1869.
John S. Perry.
Abigail M. Perkins.
Edwin C. Searles, *1857.
Caroline M. Searles, †1859.
Lucy I Seymour, †1861.
Frederic Smith, †1860.
Elizabeth Somerville, †1853.
John Stanton.
Ann Stanton.
Doras L. Stone, †1859.
Elizabeth G. Stone, †1859.
Catharine L. Tyler, †1864.
William Thresher.
Julia Trowbridge, †1856.
Charles Williams, †1855.
Sarah Williams, †1855.
Maria P. Williams, †1856.
Amelia H. Williams, †1856.
Elizabeth Williams, †1861.
Louisa B. Williams, †1861.
Calvin C. Woolworth, †1856.
Charles L. Woodbridge, †1858.
Joseph E. Woodbridge, †1859.*
Sarah E. Woodbridge, †1859.

Received in 1854.

Mary M. Barton, †1856.
Benjamin G. Barton, †1856.
Daniel H. Barton, †1856.
Augusta L. Barton, †1856.
Sarah A. Baum.
Phebe C. Black, †1856.
Samuel P. Butler, †1867.
Mary Hartwell Chittenden [Lusk].
Julia R. Clapp.
Samuel D. Crosby, †1855.
Mary N. Crosby, †1855.
Lavinia H. Crosby.
Malcolm McGregor Dana.
Robert S. Edwards, †1863.
Anna Louisa Edwards.
Helen J. Halsey, †1861.
Frances Helen Hunt, †1855.
Mary Jesup, †1856.
Charles Kellogg.
George Mygatt.

Ellen Mygatt.
Alexander Nicol, †1855.
Charlotte Rogers, *1854.
Edward Seymour.
Henry B. Sheldon, †1867.
William Warren Shumway, †1861.
Priscilla Simms, *1857.
Samuel C. Staples, †1858.
Emily T. B. Stedman, †1860.
Isaac Willard, †1859.
Frances Willis.
Cornelius Delano Wood.

Received in 1855.

Henry S. Anderson, †1860.
Jane Louisa Baldwin, †1857.
John H. Boynton, †1857.
Evelina M. W. Blunt, †1858.
Martha Butler
Ellen Ceely Cartwright.
Charity Chichester.
Phebe S. Chichester.
Cornelia B. Chittenden.
Charles B Colton, †1858.
Charles H. Dana.
Matilda L. Evans.
Samuel S. Ferris, †1859.
Francis M. Hall, *1868.
Marilla W. Hall.
Hulda Long Hall, †1868.
Jane Hamilton, *1860.
Abigail E. Hull, *1860.
Mary King [Kraus].
Henry E. Knox, †1856.
A. Augusta Lynde, †1862.
Jasper F. McChain, †1858.
Margaret McLean.
Isabel McIlvane, †1861.
Mary Caroline McIlvaine.
Margaret McPherson, †1857.
Henry Mills, †1860.
Catharine B. Mills, †1860.
Maria N. Mills, *1855.
Samuel P. Noyes.
John M. Noyes.
Fanny H. Noyes, †1859.
Horatio N. Otis, †1856.
Joseph L. Partridge, †1859.
Zibia N. Partridge, †1859.
Harriet Phillips, *1865.
Harriet C. Phillips.
Maria P Phillips.
Sarah A. Phillips.
Cornelia L. Porter.
Thomas Shand, †1862.
Rebecca Shand, †1862.

Lucy P. Sheldon, *1859.
Harriet G. Sheldon.
Benjamin S. Walcott, Jr., †1856.
Loenza B. Walcott, †1856.
Catharine French Wells.
Mary Elizabeth Wells.

Received in 1856.

Parsons P. Allen, †1861.
Elizabeth Allen, †1861.
Andrew Ayres, †1859.
Ann Eliza Ayres, †1859.
Mary A. Ayres, †1859.
Eli G. Bennett, †1861.
Grace Cain.
Lucy C. Dater, †1865.
W. Jane Dwight, *1858.
Alexander J. Emery, †1859.
Mary S. Emery, †1859.
Martha E. Emery, †1859.
Julia S. Emery [Peck], †1862.
Henry L. Francis.
Jane Goodnow.
Rhoda H. Hand.
Jeffries A. Humphrey, †1860.
Julia F. M. Humphrey, †1860.
Susan R. Hulbert, †1861.
Mary Joyce.
Catharine P. Joyce, (†1860.
Maria Bryan Lawrence [M'Ilvaine.]
Ezra Lewis, *1865.
Mary A. Mann.
Lucy R. McFarland.
Edward R. McIlvaine, †1860.
Anna Sophia Noyes, †1859.
Phebe C. Phillips.
Cynthia N. Porter, †1861.
Thomas H. Rodman, *1868.
Mary A. Rodman, *1865.
Mary Root.
Charles E. Sanford, †1858.
Ann F. Sanford, †1858.
Martha L. Smith, †1861.
Sherman H. Sterling, *1861.
Ann A. Sterling.
Julia Ann Sterling, [Baker].

Received in 1857.

Henry D. Atwater.
Eloise E. Atwood [Wood].
William Barney, †1862.
Marcia J. Berry.
Amory H. Bowman, Jr.
Asa C. Brownell.
Caroline F. Brownell.

Emeline C. Buck.
Benjamin F. Childs, †1859.
Catharine A. Dana.
Charles E. Daniels, †1862.
Charles Dunning.
John Dunning.
Alice C. Fletcher.
Mary Ferris, †1868.
Mary Anna Fleet [Kissam], †1862.
Hetty D. Gookin.
Alice E. Gray [Colton].
Charles P. Huntington, †1859.
Lucy Heustis [Potter], †1859.
Julius Ives, Jr., †1865.
Elizabeth Jackson, †1866.
Ann Julian.
Matilda R. Kent, †1863.
Isabella King [Macartney], †1866.
Albert E. Luther.
Richard Luce.
Mary Ann Luce, °1861.
Seymour Lyman, †1858.
Mary L. Lyman, †1858.
Henry F. Marsh, †1865.
Elizabeth S. Marsh, †1865.
Eliza Mason.
Emily D. Merriman [Reynolds], †1860.
N. Schuyler Moore.
Mary McMurdy, *1865.
Mary Jane Moore [Barlett], †1865.
Frances E. Mitchell.
Sarah J. Noyes, †1861.
Fanny H. Noyes, †1859.
Josephine Olmstead, *1866.
Joseph Thomas Perkins, †1865.
Charles A. Place.
James Dickinson Ripley, *1866.
Emma Sherwood [Mumby].
Jane M. Scott, †1863.
Asahel A. Shumway, †1862.
Nicholas Peck Smith.
Peter Starr.
Emma Theresa Stilwell.
Annie R. Taylor.
Sarah Louise Taylor.
Celia Jane Terry [Ferguson], †1859.
Caroline Thurston.
Ellen Thurston.
Eliza D. West, †1863.
Eliza Wild.
Charles E. Williams.
Avarilda S. Williams, *1859.
Albert C. Woodruff, †1868.
Harriet S. Woodruff.

Received in 1858.

Timothy F. Allen, *1866.

CATALOGUE OF MEMBERS.

James S. Baker, †1862.
John Barker, *1868.
David R. Barker.
Elizabeth Barker.
Eliza Berry, †1865.
Laura Berry, †1865.
Eleanor Berry [Woodruff], †1868.
Daniel M. Berry.
Phebe A. Billings, *1861.
Lucien Birdseye.
Alfred Bliss, †1861.
Elizabeth Bliss, †1861.
Maria L. Brownell [Clarke].
Nancy S. Buel, †1868.
Edwin Bulkley.
William H. Bulkley.
Lucinda W. Carter.
Martha C. Cartwright.
Irene A. Cartwright [Woodbridge].
Charlotte Chichester.
Augustus Clark, †1865.
Charles M. Clarke.
Ann Jeanette Clark, [Mrs.], *1865.
Ann Jeanette Clark, [Miss], †1865.
Josiah Colby.
Harriet E. Colby.
Jerome F. Crosby.
Lucy Collin.
Cyrus B. Davenport.
Clara Davenport [Thornton].
James P. Dike.
Camden C. Dike.
Jennie D. Dike.
Augustus M. Dickson.
John P. Duffin.
Sarah S. Duffin.
James T. Elliott.
Frederick W. Green.
Mary M. Green.
Mary L. Green [Sterling].
Deuel Goff.
Clarissa Goff.
Sidney Green.
Martica Gookin.
Agnes E. Hand, *1865.
Sarah A. Holmes, †1861.
Frank S. Holmes, †1861.
James Humphrey, †1866.
Augusta C. Hilliard, †1865.
Robert E. Jones.
Emma A. Kimberly, †1862.
Eliza Lewis.
William F. Lewis.
Joshua Leavitt, Jr.
Ann Maria Little.
John S. Mallory.
Catharine Mallory.
Elizabeth McCabb, †1861.

Caroline Mann, †1859.
D. Maria McKenzie, †1859.
John P. Mead, †1867.
Havilah Mowry.
Esther B. Mowry.
Elizabeth A. Miller [Spencer], *1860.
Cyrus Norfhup, Jr., †1866.
Edward E. Porter, *1859.
Joseph Perkins, †1860.
Louisa C. Perry.
Helen M. Phelps [Gladwin].
Mary Phelps [Woodhouse].
Eliza Ann Phelps.
Joseph Ripley.
Maria E. Sherman.
Kate A. Sherwood [Hunter].
Elizabeth Shelley, †1859.
Mary C. Starr.
Charles A. Sterling.
Sarah M. Storrs.
William C. Street.
John S. Stanton.
Walter P. Smith, *1869.
J. Nelson Tappan, †1863.
Elizabeth W. Thom.
Martha J. Thompson [Kimball], †1864.
Catharine E. M. Tarr [Bingham].
Jane Truman.
Timothy D. Vaill.
Isabella Mary Vaill.
Caroline S. Walter.
Mary W. Webster.
William A. Willard, †1861.
Thomas W. Whittemore, †1869.
Atossa Whittemore, †1869.
Juliana E. West [McMonnies], †1862.
Frederica R. West, †1862.
Mary Louise Wood.
Fanny Woodruff.
Franklin Woodruff.
Mary F. Woodruff, *1861.

Received in 1859.

Coe Adams.
Mary L. Adams.
Susan Elizabeth Barney, †1862.
Mary Barney, †1862.
Joseph D. Bates.
Margaret Brown, †1860.
Jacob R. Draper, †1865.
Julia F. Fisher [Draper], *1865.
Mary C. Fitts.
Honora Fisk.
Emily Fisk.
Nancy Ellis George, †1860.
Julia H. Holmes [Boynton], †1864.

HARRIET HULL.
ANNA HULL.
AUGUSTA W. KELLOGG.
MARGARET J. KING.
MARTHA MARY LOOMIS.
AMY MALI.
JOSEPHINE MALI [HICKS].
GEORGE H. RAND.
MARY C. RAND, *1861.
ELIZABETH SMITH, †1867.
SUSAN ELLEN SHUMWAY, †1861.

Received in 1860.

MARY J. ALLEN.
GEORGIANA LEE BARR.
EVERETT BATTELLE, *1866.
JOHN FLOYD BINGHAM.
S. ADELAIDE BINGHAM.
FLORENCE R. CLARK, †1868.
IRENE DANA, †1861.
MARTIN N. DAY.
GEORGE B. DOUGLAS.
HENRIETTA L. DOUGLAS.
SIDNEY M. GLADWIN.
GAVIN HOUSTON, †1862.
MILAN HULBERT.
CATHARINE F. HULBERT.
GEORGE E. JONES, †1861.
MALY LAMMER.
CLARISSA LAMMER.
HENRY M. MCCORKLE.
CAROLINE M. MCCORKLE.
MARTHA N. PATTEN, *1866.
THOMAS H. PEASE, †1865.
GEORGE D. PITKIN.
MAGDALEN PITKIN, *1865.
HARRIET I. RIPLEY.
CORNELIA ROGERS, †1863.
MARY SHARPE.
MARTHA A. STANLEY [WHITE], †1866.
MARY EDWARDS TAYLOR [HAYES], †1866.
CHARLES E. WEST.
ELIZABETH G. WEST, *1861.

Received in 1861.

JULIA A. ADAMS.
DOLLY H. BLAKE.
J. CARSON BREVOORT.
ELIZABETH D. BREVOORT.
MATILDA L. BURRELL.
J. Q. A. BUTLER.
ALMIRA E. BUTLER.
EMMA E. COOPER.
ISAAC M. DIMOND, *1862.
SARAH C. DIMOND [PUTNAM], †1867.
JEANETTE A. DICKINSON, †1863.

S. ALEXANDER FELTER, †1862.
ANTHONY GILKISON.
FANNY E. GILKISON.
ELLEN S. HALE, †1861.
ABIEL B. HEGEMAN.
LOUIS H. HOLMES.
ELIZABETH HOLMES, †1861.
HENRY C. HULBURT, †1861.
ANNA M. KELLOGG.
JAMES MITCHELL, †1868.
MARGARET MITCHELL, †1868.
MARGARET MCCORKLE.
GEORGE L. NICHOLS.
CHRISTINA M. NICHOLS.
MARIETTA NORTHROP, †1861.
HENRY S. OGDEN.
ANNA V. OGDEN.
CAROLINE A. SMITH.
WILLIAM VAN OLINDA.
CORNELIA M. VAN OLINDA.
CHARLES H. WATERBURY, †1866.
CATALINA W. WATERBURY, *1866.
ABBY F. WELLS.
HELEN OGDEN WOOD.
SYLVESTER WOODHOUSE.

Received in 1862.

ELLEN P. BIRDSEYE [BAYLISS].
SUSAN L. BROWN.
JAMES HENRY CAVILLE.
GEORGE COCKBURN, †1862.
MARY ELIZABETH COCKBURN, †1862.
GERTRUDE E. CUSHING [CORLY], †1866.
KATE S. DANA, †1868.
SHERWOOD B. FERRIS.
HONORA FISK [SNYDER].
HORATIO N. HOLT.
JULIUS IVES.
AMELIA IVES.
JULIA E. IVES, *1866.
ALICE A. IVES, †1866.
GERTRUDE C. IVES, †1865.
E. GRANT MARSH, †1865.
JAMES A. MARTIN.
ISAAC L. MILLER.
CHARLES L. MITCHELL, †1863.
ELIZA LEEDS MITCHELL.
CHARLES H. PAUL.
T. MELVILLE PRENTISS.
WILLIAM PRITCHARD ROBESON.
CHARLOTTE A. THURSTON.

Received in 1863.

CARLOS BARDWELL, †1865.
ORRA L. BARDWELL, †1865.

40   CATALOGUE OF MEMBERS.

Eliza Barker, *1866.
William K. Brown.
Sarah H. Brown.
Eliza H. Brown.
Jane E. Bullard.
James D. Butler, *1865.
Alexander Forman.
Amelia A. Forman.
Jacob M. Hopper.
Catharine E. Hopper.
Charles A. Hull.
Henry Hungerford.
Mary E. Hungerford.
Henry H. Irvine.
Lydia A. Irvine.
James T. Leavitt, *1868.
John Miles.
Mary B. Proctor.
Robert H. Thayer.
Hannah F. Thayer.
Augusta H. Thayer.
Sarah S. Tuthill.
Adelina S. Vail.
Joshua M. Van Cott.
Jane S. Van Cott.
Kate M. Van Cott.
Caroline S. Van Cott [Stebbins], *1868.

Received in 1864.

Augusta A. Bates.
Archibald Baxter.
Jessie Baxter.
Bridsey Blakeman, *1865.
Anna M. Blakeman, *1865.
Stephen Cahoone, Jr.
Mary Chambers, *1867.
Mary H. Cole.
Thomas H. Elfred, *1868.
Friend Palmer Fitts.
George H. Goddard.
Ralph S. Goodwin.
Rebecca Maria Hatch.
Ethel C. Hine.
Anna Humphrey.
Alice Mall.
Mary A. Merwin.
Eliza Morton.
Jane Parish.
Jemima Prentice, *1865.
Lucy C. Prentice.
Matthew P. Robbins.
Isabella J. Robbins.
Harriet Moore Stobbs.
Mary Jenks Stobbs.
Elizabeth R. Taylor.
James C. Thomas, *1868.

Abby Wells.
Charles W. West.
J. Calista Whitcomb.
Ida P. Whitcomb.
Charles L. Woodbridge.
Henry C. Woodruff.
Sarah Frances Woodruff.

Received in 1865.

John Bailey.
Samuel Barber, Jr.
Mary McKenzie Baxter.
Benjamin H. Bayliss.
Elizabeth Black.
Henry A. Blakeslee.
Euphemia J. Blakeslee.
Henry L. Brevoort.
William H. Burt.
James S. Carrigan.
David H. Cochran, *1867.
Harriet R. Cochran, *1867.
Henry R. Colby.
Margaretta Dunham.
H. Louise Dunham.
Robert Miller Elting.
Pauline Fisk.
Joseph W. Foster.
Hannah W. Foster.
Mary E. Hyde.
Harriet H. Hyde [Lowerre].
Elizabeth H. Ives.
Sarah J. Jones.
Sarah Junk.
Maria B. Lefferts.
Hannah M. P. Lewis-Bates.
Adele Mall.
Margaret Mitchell, *1868.
Harriet L. Packer.
Harriet P. Packer.
Henry Dwight Peck.
John H. Prentiss, *1866.
Edward C. Ritchie, *1868.
Martha Ritchie.
Mary Sanford.
Samuel C. Selden.
Mary Smith.
Sarah A. Smith, *1868.
Julia H. Sudam.
Clarina B. Talcott.
Nancy B. Truax.
Mary Uhlmann, *1865.
James P. Wallace.
Juliet Wallace.
Emma F. Wallace.
Charles K. Wallace, *1867.
Martha H. Wallace, *1867.

URIAH WALLACE, †1867.
JULIA WALLACE, *1867.
CHARLES A. WALLACE.
HARRIET S. WARD.
HORACE WEBSTER.

Received in 1866.

EPHRAIM E. P. ABBOTT, †1868.
JOHN F. BAKER.
WILLIAM W. BAKER.
ISABELLA CUMMING BANTER.
JOHN J. BERRY, †1868.
ALFRED E. BERRY.
CHARLOTTE A. BILLINGS.
GARIBALDO C. C. BOLOGNINI.
ARTHUR W. BRADLEY.
ELIZA S. BULL.
LUCY P. BULL.
ANNIE E. BUSHNELL.
ROBERT S. BUSSING.
MARY K. BUSSING.
ROBERT WOOD BUTLER.
JENNIE E. CHAMBERLIN.
SIMEON B. CRITTENDEN, JR.
WILLIAM H. CHURCHILL.
FERRIS W. COLBY, †1868.
FREDERICK H. COLTON.
DANIEL F. COMSTOCK.
EMILY Y. COMSTOCK
DAVID Y. COMSTOCK.
ALONZO CRITTENDEN.
MARY W. CRITTENDEN.
EDWARD W. CRITTENDEN.
FRANK DANA.
ROBERT KNIGHT DANA.
DANNIEL DENNIS.
WILLIAM S. DUNHAM.
MARY E. DUNNE.
JOHN A. FRENCH.
EDWARD P. GILBERT.
ALMIRA L. GILBERT.
FREDERICK M. GREEN.
CAROLINE A. GREEN.
MARY DEMING GREEN.
MARY R. GRIFFITH.
HORACE C. HARDY.
CLARA C. HARRISON.
EMMA HAWKINS.
GEORGE L. HULL.
ELLEN HUMPHREY.
HETTIE WAKEMAN JESSUP.
WILLIAM TUCKER JOHNSON.
ELIZABETH S. LANE.
HARRIET LEWIS.
SARAH M. LOW.
JANE E. LUDLOW.

EDWARD J. MAXWELL, †1866.
PETER McCARTEE.
ANNA J. McCARTEE.
CORNELIA A. McCLURE, *1867.
CHARLOTTE M. MITCHELL.
LISETTE MONTMOLLIN.
GEORGE W. MOORE.
ABBY C. NELSON, †1867.
EMMA R. NORTON.
TAMISON H. PARSONS.
MARY S. PECK
HENRY M. PECKHAM.
SUSAN PECKHAM.
JOHN H. PRENTICE.
SARAH M. PRENTICE.
ELLEN PRENTICE.
EMMA C. PRENTICE.
MARY HILL PRENTICE.
MARTHA H. PRENTICE.
HENRY GREGORY RAND.
BLANCHE LOUISE READ.
SARAH FLORENCE READ.
HARRIET W. ROBINSON.
MARY R. SANFORD [HATCH].
CELIA SEEBER, †1867.
CLEMENT SHARPE.
CATHARINE M. SCRIMGEOUR
JAMES SHELDON.
LOUISA S. SHERMAN [LOUD].
SARAH H. SMITH.
ELIZABETH A. STANTON.
KATE LOUISE STANTON.
ADELINE W. STERLING.
VIRGINIA S. STERLING.
HENRY STEVENS.
ARTHUR STEVENS.
MARY E. STRANGE.
GEORGE E. THURSTON.
ANTOINETTE A. TOWNSEND.
SARAH TOWNSEND.
EDGAR TUCKER.
MARY P. TUCKER.
HANNAH W. TUCKER.
HULDA B. TUTHILL.
JENNIE E. VAN COTT.
CALEB G. WEAVER.
HARRIETTA S. WEAVER.
CAROLINE ISABEL WEAVER
ELIZABETH G. WEST.
VIOLA M. WHIGHAM, †1869.
PHEBE J. WOODRUFF.
EVA MARIA WILFORD.

Received in 1867.

WILLIAM ANDERSON
MARY ANDERSON.

SAUMEL BARBER.
ANN BARBER.
EMILY C. BARBER [CAMPBELL].
MARY LOUISE BARBER.
DAVID B. BAYLIS.
MARY L. BAYLIS.
EMMA BLACKWOOD.
A. ISABEL BROWN.
ALONZO CALKINS.
SALTER STORRS CLARK.
SAMUEL C. DARLING, [1867]
JOHN G. DEANE.
WATSON B. DICKERMAN.
JEANIE DOUGLASS.
AUGUSTUS R. S. FOOTE.
ELIZA O. FORREST.
MARGARET FORREST [YOUNG].
THOMAS FORREST.
CHARLES H. GIBERSON.
RICHARD GRAVES, JR.
THEODORE HINSDALE.
GRACE WEBSTER HINSDALE.
WILLIAM H HUMPHREY.
GERTRUDE I. JAMES.
JOHN EDWARD JOHNSON.
FANNY H. LEFFINGWELL.
THOMAS F. PHIPPS.
FRANCES A. PUTNAM.
CHARLES C. PUTNAM
ELSIETTE STAFFORD.
LEILA STAFFORD.
GEORGE P. STOCKWELL.
CAROLINE O. STOCKWELL.
ELIZA STRATTON.
EMMA A. STRATTON.
MARTHA E. SWIFT [DICKERMAN].
ABBIE M. THOMPSON.
MARY W. WARNER.
DAVID WESSON.
ALICE G. WESSON.

Received in 1868.

ALBERT G. ALLEN, JR.
BESSIE ALLEN.
E. ALMENA BROWN.
KATE R. BOYCE.
PHEBE CROSBY.
LUCY FAYERWEATHER.
AUGUSTA DWIGHT FERRIS.
FREDERICK R. FOWLER.
SARAH P. FOWLER.
CHARLES L. W. GREENWOOD.
WILLIAM P. HOWLAND, JR.
D. A. KNOWLTON.
EVELINE KNOWLTON.
CHARLES P. LOW.
ARTHUR MATHEWSON.
ELIZABETH H. REMINGTON.
JAMES RICE.
SARAH E. RICE.
JAMES RICE, JR.
MARGARETT LANMAN ROBINSON.
CASSIUS M. TERRY.

Received, January, 1869.

DEBORAH ANN BRIGGS.
ASA COOK BROWNELL, JR.
ANNA L. BROWNELL.
CAROLINE R. BROWNELL.
SARAH S. CROMWELL.
MARY HILL CHITTENDEN.
AUBREY G. HUTCHESON.
ANNA B. HUTCHESON.
HORACE MAXWELL.
WILLIAM F. MERRILL.
JULIA A. MERRILL.
DONALD McLEOD.
JOSEPHINE FLORENCE PAUL.
FRANCES A. PITKIN.
MARY B. PHILLIPS.
DAVID SMART.
CORNELIA B. WILLIAMS

Alphabetical List of Present Members.

Aborn, Charles B.
Ackley, Edward F.
Adams, Calvin.
Adams, Julia A.
Adams, Coe.
Adams, Mary L.
Allen, Albert G.
Allen, Lucy W.
Allen, Albert G., Jr.
Allen, Bessie.
Allen, Mary J.
Anderson, William.
Anderson, Mary.
Atkinson, Charles M.
Atwater, James C.
Atwater, Christina S.
Atwater, Henry D.

Bailey, John.
Bailey, William E.
Baker, William W.
Baker, Julia S.
Baker, John F.
Barber, Samuel.
Barber, Ann.
Barber, Samuel, Jr.
Barber, Mary Louise.
Barker, David R.
Barker, Elizabeth.
Barnes, John C.
Barnes, Mary S.
Barr, Georgiana Lee.
Bates, Joseph D.
Bates, Hannah M. L.
Bates, Augusta A.
Baum, Sarah A.
Baylis, David B.
Baylis, Mary L.
Bayliss, Benjamin H.
Bayliss, Ellen P.
Bayliss, Sarah.
Baxter, Archibald.
Baxter, Jessie.
Baxter, Mary McKenzie.
Baxter, Isabella Cumming.

Berry, Daniel M.
Berry, Marcia J.
Berry, Alfred E.
Billings, Charlotte A.
Bingham, S. Adelaide.
Bingham, John Floyd.
Bingham, Catharine E. M.
Birdseye, Lucien.
Birdseye, Catharine M.
Black, Elizabeth.
Blackwood, Emma.
Blake, Dolly H.
Blakeslee, Henry A.
Blakeslee, Euphemia J.
Bolognini, Garibaldo C. C.
Bowman, Amory H., Jr.
Bradley, Arthur W.
Brevoort, J. Carson.
Brevoort, Elizabeth D.
Brevoort, Henry L.
Boyce, Kate R.
Briggs, Deborah Ann.
Brown, Chauncey W.
Brown, Susan L.
Brown, William K.
Brown, Sarah H.
Brown, Eliza H.
Brown, A. Isabel.
Brown, E. Almena.
Brownell, Asa C.
Brownell, Caroline F.
Brownell, Anna L.
Brownell, Caroline R.
Brownell, Asa Cook, Jr.
Buck, Richard P.
Buck, Charlotte.
Buck, Emeline C.
Bulkeley, William H.
Bulkeley, Julia.
Bulkley, Edwin.
Bulkley, Helen.
Bull, Eliza S.
Bull, Lucy P.
Bullard, Jane E.
Burrall, Frederick A.
Burrill, Elizabeth G.

Burrill, Catharine H.
Burrell, Matilda L.
Burt, William H.
Bushnell, Annie E.
Bussing, Robert S.
Bussing, Mary K.
Butler, Martha.
Butler, John Q. A.
Butler, Almira E.
Butler, Robert Wood.

Cahoone, Stephen, Jr.
Cain, Grace.
Cain, Margaret A.
Caldwell, Charles B.
Calkins, Alonzo.
Campbell, Emily B.
Carrigan, James S.
Carter, Lucinda W.
Cartwright, Emily R.
Cartwright, Ellen Ceely.
Cartwright, Martha C.
Caville, James Henry.
Chamberlin, Jennie E.
Chichester, Charity.
Chichester, Phebe S.
Chichester, Charlotte.
Chittenden, Simeon B.
Chittenden, Cornelia B.
Chittenden, Anna H.
Chittenden, Simeon B., Jr.
Chittenden, Mary Hill.
Church, Robert.
Church, Eliza James.
Churchill, William H.
Clapp, Clinton.
Clapp, Julia R.
Clark, Salter Storrs.
Clarke, Charles M.
Clarke, Maria L.
Colby, Josiah.
Colby, Harriet E.
Colby, Henry R.
Cole, Mary H.
Collin, Lucy.
Colton, Frederick H.
Colton, Alice G.
Comstock, David F.
Comstock, Emily Y.
Comstock, David Y.
Cooper, Emma E.
Creech, Ellen H.
Crittenden, Alonzo.
Crittenden, Mary W.
Crittenden, Edward W.
Cromwell, Sarah S.
Crosby, Jerome F.

Crosby, Lavinia H.
Crosby, Phebe.
Crozier, Isabella.

Dana, Francis E.
Dana, Malcolm McGregor.
Dana, Catharine A.
Dana, Charles H.
Dana, Frank.
Dana, Robert Knight.
Day, Martin N.
Davenport, Cyrus B.
Deane, John G.
Dennis, Daniel.
Dickerman, Watson B.
Dickerman, Martha E.
Dickson, Augustus M.
Dike, James P.
Dike, Harriet A.
Dike, Camden C.
Dike, Jennie D.
Dixon, Anna.
Douglass, Jeanie.
Douglass, Thomas.
Douglass, Laura.
Douglas, George B.
Douglas, Henrietta L.
Duffin, John P.
Duffin, Sarah S.
Dunham, William S.
Dunham, Margaretta.
Dunham, H. Louise.
Dunne, Mary E.
Dunning, Charles.
Dunning, John.

Edwards, Anna Louisa.
Elliott, James T.
Elting, Robert Miller.
Evans, Matilda L.

Fayerweather, Lucy.
Ferris, Sherwood B.
Ferris, Augusta Dwight.
Fisher, Francis.
Fisk, Honora.
Fisk, Emily.
Fisk, Pauline.
Fitts, Friend P.
Fitts, Mary C.
Fletcher, Alice C.
Foote, Augustus R. S.
Forman, Alexander.
Forman, Amelia A.
Forrest, Eliza O.
Forrest, Thomas.
Foster, Joseph W.

FOSTER, HANNAH W.
FOWLER, FREDERICK R.
FOWLER, SARAH P.
FOX, ARETHUSA J.
FRANCIS, HENRY L.
FRENCH, JOHN A.

GARDINER, OLIVER C.
GARDINER, L. ADELINE.
GIBERSON, CHARLES H.
GILBERT, EDWARD R.
GILBERT, ALMIRA L.
GILKISON, ANTHONY.
GILKISON, FANNY E.
GLADWIN, SIDNEY M.
GLADWIN, HELEN M.
GODDARD, GEORGE H
GOOCH, ELIZABETH L.
GOODNOW, A. FRANKLIN.
GOODNOW, JANE.
GOODMAN, STEPHEN S.
GOODWIN, RALPH S.
GOFF, DEUEL.
GOFF, CLARISSA.
GOOKIN, HETTY D.
GOOKIN, MARTICA.
GRAVES, RICHARD, JR.
GRAY, SARAH H.
GREEN, FREDERICK W.
GREEN, MARY M.
GREEN, CAROLINE A.
GREEN, SIDNEY.
GREEN, MARY R.
GREEN, MARY DEMING.
GREEN, FREDERICK M.
GREENWOOD, CHARLES L. W.
GRIFFITH, MARY R.

HALL, MARILLA W.
HAND, RHODA H.
HARDY, HORACE C.
HARRISON, CLARA C.
HATCH, WALTER T.
HATCH, REBECCA T.
HATCH, REBECCA MARIA.
HATCH, MARY S.
HAWES, WELLES.
HAWES, ANGELICA A.
HAWKINS, EMMA.
HEGEMAN, ABIEL B.
HICKS, JOSEPHINE M.
HINDS, MARIA.
HINE, ETHEL C.
HINSDALE, THEODORE.
HINSDALE, GRACE WEBSTER.
HOFFMANN, LAURA S.

HOLT, HORATIO N.
HOLMES, LOUIS H.
HOPPER, JACOB M.
HOPPER, CATHARINE E.
HOWLAND, WILLIAM P., JR.
HULBERT, MILAN.
HULBERT, CATHARINE F.
HULL, AURELIUS B.
HULL, SARAH T.
HULL, CHARLES A.
HULL, GEORGE L.
HULL, HARRIET.
HULL, ANNA.
HUMPHREY, URANIA.
HUMPHREY, ELLEN.
HUMPHREY, ANNA.
HUMPHREY, WILLIAM H.
HUNGERFORD, HENRY.
HUNGERFORD, MARY E.
HUNTINGTON, JOSHUA.
HUNTER, KATE S.
HUTCHESON, AUBREY G.
HUTCHESON, ANNA B.
HYDE, MARIANNE.
HYDE, MARY E.

IRVINE, HENRY H.
IRVINE, LYDIA A.
IVES, JULIUS.
IVES, AMELIA.
IVES, ELIZABETH H.

JAMES, MARY J.
JAMES, GERTRUDE L.
JESSUP, HATTIE WAKEMAN.
JOHNSON, DWIGHT.
JOHNSON, MARY T.
JOHNSON, WILLIAM TUCKER.
JOHNSON, JOHN EDWARD.
JOHNSON, SARAH E.
JONES, ROBERT E.
JONES, PRISCILLA H.
JONES, SARAH J.
JOYCE, MARY.
JOYCE, CATHARINE P.
JULIAN, ANN.
JUNK, SARAH.

KELLOGG, CHARLES.
KELLOGG, AUGUSTA W.
KELLOGG, ANNA M.
KING, HARRIET.
KING, MARGARET J.
KNOWLTON, D. A.
KNOWLTON, EVELINE.

KRAUS, MARY K.

LAMMER, MARY.
LAMMER, CLARISSA.
LANE, ELIZABETH S.
LEAVITT, MARY URSULA.
LEAVITT, JOSHUA
LEAVITT, SARAH.
LEAVITT, JOSHUA, JR.
LEFFERTS, MARIA B.
LEFFINGWELL, FANNY H.
LEWIS, HARRIET.
LEWIS, ELIZA.
LEWIS, WILLIAM F.
LITTLE, ANN MARIA.
LOOMIS, MARTHA MARY.
LOUD, LOUISA S.
LOW, CHARLES P.
LOW, SARAH M.
LOWEREE, HARRIET H.
LUCE, RICHARD.
LUDLOW, JANE E.
LUSK, MARY H. C.
LUTHER, ALBERT E.

MALL, AMY.
MALL, ALICE.
MALL, ADELE.
MALLORY, JOHN S.
MALLORY, CATHARINE.
MANN, MARY A.
MARSH, FRANCES.
MARSH, MARY B.
MARSH, LAURA L.
MARTIN, JAMES A.
MASON, ELIZA.
MATHEWSON, ARTHUR.
MAXWELL, HORACE.
MCCARTEE, PETER.
MCCARTEE, ANNA J.
MCCORKLE, HENRY M.
MCCORKLE, CAROLINE M.
MCCORKLE, MARGARET.
MCFARLAND, LUCY R.
MCILVAINE, MARY CAROLINE.
MCLEAN, MARGARET.
MCLEOD, DONALD.
MERRILL, WILLIAM F.
MERRILL, JULIA A.
MERWIN, MARY.
MILES, JOHN.
MILLER, ISAAC L.
MITCHELL, CHAUNCEY L.
MITCHELL, FRANCES E.
MITCHELL, ELIZA L.
MITCHELL, CHARLOTTE M.
MONTMOLLIN, LISETTE.

MOORE, CHAUNCEY W.
MOORE, CLARA.
MOORE, N. SCHUYLER.
MOORE, GEORGE W.
MORTON, ELIZA.
MOWRY, HAVILAH.
MOWRY, ESTHER B.
MUMBY, EMMA S.
MYGATT, ELI, JR.
MYGATT, SOPHIA.
MYGATT, GEORGE.
MYGATT, ELLEN.

NICHOLS, GEORGE L.
NICHOLS, CHRISTINA M.
NORTON, EMMA R.
NOYES, MARY JANE.
NOYES, SAMUEL.
NOYES, HENRIETTA J.
NOYES, JOHN M.
NOYES, SAMUEL P.

OGDEN, HENRY S.
OGDEN, ANNA A.
OLMSTEAD, MARY A.

PACKER, HARRIET L.
PACKER, HARRIET P.
PARISH, JANE.
PARSONS, TAMISON H.
PAUL, CHARLES M.
PAUL, JOSEPHINE FLORENCE
PECK, WILLIAM M.
PECK, ELIZA.
PECK, HENRY DWIGHT.
PECK, MARY S.
PECKHAM, HENRY M.
PECKHAM, SUSAN.
PERKINS, ABIGAIL M.
PERRY, ROBERT.
PERRY, MARY S.
PERRY, LOUISA C.
PERRY, JOHN S.
PHELPS, SAMUEL F.
PHELPS, PHEBE.
PHELPS, ELIZA ANN.
PHELPS, MARY B.
PHILLIPS, HARRIET C.
PHILLIPS, MARIA P.
PHILLIPS, SARAH A.
PHILLIPS, PHEBE C.
PHIPPS, THOMAS F.
PITKIN, GEORGE D.
PITKIN, FRANCES A.
PLACE, CHARLES.
PORTER, ALFRED H.
PORTER, CORNELIA C.

PORTER, CORNELIA L.
PRENTICE, JOHN H.
PRENTICE, SARAH M.
PRENTICE, ELLEN.
PRENTICE, EMMA C.
PRENTICE, MARY HILL.
PRENTICE, MARTHA H.
PRENTICE, LUCY C.
PRENTISS, T. MELVILLE.
PRICE, MARGARET.
PROCTOR, MARY B.
PUTNAM, FRANCES A.
PUTNAM, CHARLES C.

RAND, GEORGE H.
RAND, HENRY GREGORY.
READ, BLANCHE LOUISE.
READ, SARAH FLORENCE.
REID, MARTHA.
REMINGTON, ELIZABETH H.
RICE, JAMES.
RICE, SARAH E.
RICE, JAMES, JR.
RICHARDSON, ELLEN M. P.
RIPLEY, JOSEPH.
RIPLEY, ELIZA C.
RIPLEY, HARRIET I.
RITCHIE, MARTHA.
ROBBINS, MATTHEW P.
ROBBINS, ISABELLA J.
ROBESON, WILLIAM PRITCHARD.
ROBINSON, JEREMIAH P.
ROBINSON, ELIZABETH.
ROBINSON, HARRIET W.
ROBINSON, MARGARETT LANMAN.
ROCKWELL, MARY D.
ROOT, MARY.

SANDERSON, SIDNEY.
SANDERSON, MARY A.
SANDERSON, ABIGAIL J.
SANFORD, MARY.
SCHIMGEOUR, CATHARINE M.
SELDEN, SAMUEL C.
SEYMOUR, EDWARD.
SHARPE, HEZEKIAH D.
SHARPE, ELIZABETH A.
SHARPE, MARY.
SHARPE, CLEMENT.
SHELDON, JAMES.
SHELDON, HARRIET G.
SHERMAN, BENJAMIN P.
SHERMAN, MARIA E.
SMART, DAVID.
SMITH, CAROLINE A.
SMITH, ELIZABETH J.

SMITH, MARY.
SMITH, MARY.
SMITH, SARAH H.
SMITH, NICHOLAS PECK.
SMYTHE, LOUISE G.
SNOW, LORENZO.
SNOW, JULIET E.
SNOW, JANE.
SNYDER, HONORA F.
STAFFORD, ELSIETTE.
STAFFORD, LEILA.
STANTON, LUCY JANE.
STANTON, JOHN S.
STANTON, GEORGE A.
STANTON, ELIZABETH A.
STANTON, KATE LOUISE.
STANTON, JOHN.
STANTON, ANN.
STARR, PETER.
STARR, MARY C.
STERLING, ANN A.
STERLING, ADELINE W.
STERLING, VIRGINIA S.
STERLING, CHARLES A.
STERLING, MARY L.
STEVENS, HENRY.
STEVENS, ARTHUR.
STEWART, SARAH.
STEWART, ANN.
STILWELL, EMMA THERESA.
STOCKWELL, GEORGE P.
STOCKWELL, CAROLINE O.
STORRS, RICHARD S., JR.
STORRS, MARY ELWELL.
STORRS, HARRIET MOORE.
STORRS, MARY JENKS.
STORRS, JAMES H.
STORRS, SUSAN F.
STORRS, CHARLES.
STORRS, MARYETT M.
STORRS, SARAH M.
STRANGE, MARY E.
STRATTON, ELIZA.
STRATTON, EMMA A.
STREET, WILLIAM C.
SUYDAM, JULIA H.
SWIFT, CATHARINE E.

TALCOTT, CLARINA B.
TAPPAN, SUSAN STOREY.
TAYLOR, ANNIE R.
TAYLOR, SARAH LOUISE.
TAYLOR, ELIZABETH R.
TERRY, CASSIUS M.
THAYER, ROBERT H.
THAYER, HANNAH F.

THAYER, AUGUSTA H.
THOMAS, MARQUIS D.
THOMAS, LYDIA.
THOMAS, AMELIA E.
THOMPSON, ABBIE M.
THORNTON, CLARA D.
THRESHER, WILLIAM.
THOM, ELIZABETH W.
THURSTON, CAROLINE.
THURSTON, ELLEN.
THURSTON, GEORGE E.
THURSTON, CHARLOTTE A.
TOWNSEND, ANTOINETTE A.
TOWNSEND, SARAH.
TRUAX, NANCY B.
TRUMAN, JANE.
TUCKER, EDGAR.
TUCKER, MARY P.
TUCKER, HANNAH W.
TUTHILL, HULDA B.
TUTHILL, SARAH S.

VAIL, ADELINA S.
VAILL, TIMOTHY D.
VAILL, ISABELLA MARY.
VAN COTT, JOSHUA M.
VAN COTT, JANE S.
VAN COTT, KATE M.
VAN COTT, JENNIE E.
VAN OLINDA, WILLIAM.
VAN OLINDA, CORNELIA M.

WALLACE, JAMES P.
WALLACE, JULIET.
WALLACE, EMMA F.
WALLACE, CHARLES A.
WALTER, CAROLINE S.
WARD, HARRIET S.
WARNER, MARY W.
WEAVER, CALEB G.
WEAVER, HARRIETTA S.

WEAVER, CAROLINE ISABEL.
WEBSTER, HORACE.
WEBSTER, MARY W.
WELLS, ABBY T.
WELLS, ABBY.
WELLS, CATHARINE FRENCH.
WELLS, MARY ELIZABETH
WESSON, DAVID.
WESSON, ALICE G.
WEST, CHARLES E.
WEST, CHARLES W.
WEST, ELIZABETH G.
WHEELWRIGHT, MARY N.
WHITCOMB, J. CALISTA.
WHITCOMB, IDA P.
WILD, ELIZA.
WILLIAMS, CHARLES E.
WILLIAMS, CORNELIA B.
WILLIAMS, MARTIN H.
WILLIS, FRANCES.
WOOD, ELOISE A.
WOOD, CORNELIUS DELANO.
WOOD, HELEN OGDEN.
WOOD, MARY LOUISE.
WOODBRIDGE, CHARLES L.
WOODBRIDGE, IRENE A.
WOODHOUSE, SYLVESTER L.
WOODHOUSE, MARY P.
WOODRUFF, ALBERT.
WOODRUFF, HARRIET.
WOODRUFF, CYNTHIA.
WOODRUFF, FANNY.
WOODRUFF, HARRIET S.
WOODRUFF, HENRY C.
WOODRUFF, SARAH F.
WOODRUFF, FRANKLIN.
WOODRUFF, PHEBE J.
WREFORD, EVA MARIA.
WYMAN, WILLIAM H.

YOUNG, MARGARET F.

www.ingramcontent.com/pod-product-compliance
Lightning Source LLC
Chambersburg PA
CBHW020257090426
4273SCB00009B/1122